GHETTO

Fifty years have passed since the beginning of World War II. But there are some things which can and should never be forgotten.

On 15 November 1940 half a million people were sealed within the Warsaw Ghetto. It was the first step towards their extermination.

Very few people lived to bear witness; but written words live on. The diaries and papers which survived bear witness to a basic human hope: that those who cry in the night will be heard beyond the dark.

This book is intended neither to moralize nor to theorize, but simply to allow eyewitnesses to speak.

'These poems, written because I have walked where the Ghetto once stood, distil the pain and loss I sensed. I have tried to give voice to those who were silenced, to make a memorial kaddish, to light a frail candle flame: because we need to mourn and not to forget.'

JENNY ROBERTSON is the author of a number of books of poetry as well as novels and plays. Her life-long love of Poland, its language, literature and people stems from student years when she worked among Nazi victims in displaced persons camps. She then did postgraduate studies in Warsaw where the tragedy of the Holocaust became deeply imprinted in her experience.

GHETTO

Poems of the Warsaw Ghetto 1939–43

JENNY ROBERTSON

A LION PAPERBACK
Oxford · Batavia · Sydney

Copyright © 1989 Jenny Robertson

Published by
Lion Publishing plc
Sandy Lane West, Littlemore, Oxford, England
ISBN 0 7459 1804 2
Lion Publishing Corporation
1705 Hubbard Avenue, Batavia, Illinois 60510, USA
ISBN 0 7459 1804 2
Albatross Books Pty Ltd
PO Box 320, Sutherland, NSW 2232, Australia
ISBN 0 7324 0146 1

First edition 1989

Acknowledgments
The prayer from Ravensbruck is reproduced by permission from Sue Ryder,
Child of My Love, Collins Harvill, 1986

British Library Cataloguing in Publication Data
Robertson, Jenny
  Ghetto: poems of the Warsaw Ghetto, 1939—43.
  I. Title
  821'.914

  ISBN 0-7459-1804-2

Library of Congress Cataloging-in-Publication Data
Robertson, Jenny.
  Ghetto: poems of the Warsaw Ghetto, 1939—43/Jenny Robertson. — 1st ed.
  p.   cm. — (A Lion paperback)
  ISBN 0-7459-1804-2
  1. Holocaust, Jewish (1939—45)—Poland—Warsaw—Poetry.
  2. Jews—Poland—Warsaw—Poetry.   3. Warsaw (Poland)—History—
  —Poetry.   I. Title.
  PR6068.0184G4   1989
  821'.914—dc20

Printed in Great Britain by Cox and Wyman Ltd, Reading

O LORD, remember not only the men and women of goodwill but also those of illwill.
But do not only remember all the suffering they have inflicted on us, remember the fruits we bought, thanks to this suffering, our comradeship, our loyalty, our humility, the courage, the generosity, the greatness of heart which has grown out of all this, and when they come to judgment, let all the fruits that we have borne be their forgiveness.

This prayer was found on a piece of wrapping paper near the body of a dead child in Ravensbruck Nazi concentration camp, where 92,000 women and children died.

CONTENTS

INTRODUCTION

On 15 November 1941 half a million people were sealed
within the Warsaw Ghetto. No one knew what lay ahead.
For some the new situation, cramped and inconvenient,
brought, initially, a false sense of safety. For others it was
reassuring, even a sign of hope, to see for the first time young
Jewish policemen in the overcrowded streets. But their
sealing-off was the first step towards their extermination.

Starvation, epidemics, random killings, and suicide
quickly took their toll, but in July 1942 new measures were
taken: deportation 'further east' — to newly-constructed gas
chambers in Treblinka, a mere sixty kilometres away.

In May 1943, after heroic resistance, Poland's largest
ghetto was liquidated.

Classified as subhuman, hunted off the face of the
earth, a few survivors took refuge where they could. Only
one per cent of the original half million lived to bear
witness; but written words live on. Painstakingly, in ever
worsening circumstances, people kept detailed diaries,
which they entrusted to Gentile friends, or simply buried.
Their work testifies to a basic human hope: that those who
cry in the night will be heard beyond the dark.

These poems, written because I have walked where the
Ghetto once stood, distil the pain and loss I sensed beyond
housing blocks, beyond houses and churches carefully
reconstructed in their former style. I have tried to give voice
to those who were silenced, to make a memorial kaddish, to
light a frail candle flame: because we need to mourn and
not forget.

JENNY ROBERTSON

PRELUDE

MEANING OF PAIN

'If you wish to know the meaning of your pain,
you must yourself become that pain's revealer'
ABRAHAM SUTZKEVER[1]

Night. No time for heroes, only base,
essential craft — deceit. Each stratagem
delineates boundaries we feel forced
to break. Survival is the end
which justifies. Should this surprise?
Protest is nothing else than suicide.

BETWEEN THE FLAME AND THE ASH

Let years roll back to 1943.
A note deplores 'the whole world's apathy.
I pen this with my life. S. Zygelboim.
In Paris, Wien, in London you are dumb.
You watch my people die, do not protest.
I give those dead my death. I've nothing left.'

The year before in Warsaw, when the plan's
outlined, Adam Czerniakow will not sign
this order for selection, genocide;
dare not resist, and swallows cyanide.

Though death awaits at last each one of us
we tremble at this calculated stroke.
Black smoke spells out the Aryan joke:
Queue, naked Jew, for showers — and find gas.

The words of this poem's title are by Carol
Rumens.[2]
Shmuel Zygelboim,[3] a member of the Polish
National Council, took his own life in London,
on 11 May 1943, as an act of protest against world
indifference at the destruction of Polish Jewry,
leaving the message quoted in the poem. Adam
Czerniakow[4] headed the Ghetto *Judenrat*. He
refused to sign the documents authorizing the
deportation of Ghetto dwellers 'further east'.

NIGHT

Night. As early as the twenties
Isaac Babel[1] foresees the end,
creates a play
around the change from man of property
to hollow automaton, a robot forced to bend
to thugs and upstarts, while people pray —
observe old ritual, but lose the inner sense.
'Ich dank dir Gott, az ich bin a id.'
Later the cry will be:
                    'Ich dank — az ich bin . . . '
when everyone else has ceased to be,
when nightfall brings more terrors than the day,
when hunger strikes as hard as the S.S.
and selection becomes a pseudonym for death.
                    Bshono haba b' jerushalaim.

'Ich dank dir, Gott . . . ': words of a Yiddish folk song. Nuchem
Lejbkorn, a prosperous householder, was quickly reduced to
poverty in the Ghetto. His wife and eldest child died of typhus in
the same week. This blow turned Lejbkorn into an idiot. With his
remaining four children he spent his days begging, singing the only
song he knew.
The incident is recorded by Samuel Puterman,[2] who survived the
Ghetto, and the 1944 Warsaw Uprising. He was arrested and taken
to Sachsenhausen and Orianburg. After the war he returned to
Warsaw, but later left for France. He donated his memoirs to the
Jewish Historical Archives. The poem 'Geipel' is also taken from
Puterman's account.

LULLABY

Lullaby. Hear the golden goat cry:
Almonds for sale:
Raisins[1] and almonds fresh from the tree.
Hush now, don't wail . . .
Here are almonds for you and raisins for me.

Sleep, Jewish child.
Smoke always chokes least
when the wind's in the east.
How still those bairns lie!
Dream raisins and nuts.
The golden goat's cry
ends where a bright ladder touches the sky.
Sleep, sleep, hush-a-bye.

The sun is smiling in the sky.
I'm ten years old. I will not die,
I'd like to go back home again.
Yet every day
transports take our friends away.

B'shona haba b' jerushalaim.

TIGHTROPE WALKER

A painting by Gabriella Freiova

Let's all hold hands — it's safer so. Now try
to walk a tightrope stretched against the sky.
Don't lose your balance, please, don't fall, for no
nice safety net is waiting down below.
There's nothing left except this length of rope.
Hold your head high. It is our only hope.
The Ghetto walls don't keep the death trains out —
and even those who guess that gas awaits
think silence is the kindest way to care,
keep starving, homesick children from despair.

So Gabriella works with paints, engrossed,
forgets the feel of hunger, pain and loss.
She is eleven now, and it is May.
Next week she's turned to ashes, blown away.

Gabriella Freiova was born in 1933. She lived in group 3,
hut 13 in the Czech Ghetto, Terezin. She painted her
picture 'Tightrope Walker' on 10 May 1944, and was
transported to Auschwitz two days later.

A WAVE OF BENEDICTION[1]

'We weep later, in full sunlight,
never at the precise moment.'
OSCAR MILOSZ

Light, a wave of benediction
washes the evening sky.
We are all implicated,
we, the ones who did not die;
we, the then unborn,
who grew to learn
the meaning of the six-pointed star.[2]

The fires have gone out
all over Europe,
and we are cold.
Our tragedy — to have ignored;
our loss — that we refused to know,
even that medieval Jewry had been put to flight,
or that waves of later hatred brought them west
from Odessa and Lublin to sew shirts
in London, set up a stall in Leeds,
(nothing more than sixpence
or less than a penny here).
From Vilnius to Glasgow
from the Niemen to New York
(but never to York in England,
scene of a Crusading massacre,
never there).

ICH WEISS NICHT

The flame, though bright, seemed foreign.
We did not stretch out our hands,
despised the rock from which was hewn
the knowledge of the Nameless,
hope of justice for the poor.
Who fasts now at Yom Kippur?

Ich weiss es nicht.

Ich weiss nicht, was soll es bedeuten,
Dass ich so traurig bin:
Ein Maerchen aus alten Zeiten,
Das kommt mir nicht aus dem Sinn.

From childhood I cut threads to make this poem:
I knew no Hebrew, little Scripture, save
the foreign woman, Ruth's, entreaty,
Thy people and thy God belong to me.[1]

I admired that Gentile woman's loyalty,
revelled in her great grandson's wild lament,
and all the passion of its anguished poetry.
The beauty of Israel is slain.[2]

Later, came walks beside a cemetery
where stones carved in the heavy shapes of Hebrew
were crowded close together; and no flowers grew.

Yom Kippur is the Feast of Atonement. Nazi action against the Jews
was often targetted to coincide with major religious feasts. I have
quoted from 'Die Lorelei', because Heinrich Heine, the author, is
Jewish. It also shows that the Judaic-Christian tradition shares
important sources and roots which have nurtured our cultures and
world view.

'HOW OLD WAS I . . . ?'

How old was I when I first heard of Auschwitz?
I do not know; perhaps knew first
that a Dutch schoolgirl was kept hidden,
that Shylock laughs when he is tickled,
that King John drew
teeth, Pharaoh exploited Hebrews,
while Herod's soldiers slew,
like Pharaoh, Jewish babies —
but that was long ago;
and from the Egyptian murders
came exodus, a freeing of the slaves;
from the English, Magna Carta;
while Herod's slaughter saved the infant Jesus.

           So I read a happy ending
           into the ancient stories
           as children like to do.

THE DEAD

We hold within ourselves
shadowy beings
of no seeming relevance —
except that survival depends
on remembering.

They gave us life.
We once slept, unseen, within.
Now — and this is their bequeathing —
we continue their uncharted path
long after memories fade,
more frail than ash.

MEDIEVAL GHETTOS

*'Ido vocabatur getto,
quia erant ibi ultra duodecim fornaces
et ibi fundabatur aes.'*
SENATE OF VENICE

Beside the furnace, yawning fire of hell,
the Venice Senate marks out 'Lebensraum':
where copper once was forged, now Jews must dwell.

In Aragon the Hebrews are controlled;
Ferrara, Frankfurt, ghettos become homes;
for Christendom deems Jews are doomed to hell.

On Eve of Av Pope Paul rings out his bell,
creates a street for Jews in Christian Rome,
on Tiber's bank two thousand Hebrews dwell.

In cramped surroundings, schools and theatres tell
that learning flourished lacking doge or dome
beside the furnace, yawning fire of hell

till liberty proclaims its world-wide call:
belief is free, ghettos are overthrown.
Where copper once was forged no Jew need dwell.

The Nurenberg decrees exclude, expel.
New ghettos rise, essential rights disowned.
Beside the furnace Jews are marked for hell;
where death is forged, despair and madness dwell.

PYRAMID OF POWER

Myth

named Adolf

a race of Aryans of the purest blood

all   white   races   except   the   Slavs

Slavs, gypsies, undesirables, defective or dark-skinned,

typhoid fever, TB, ghetto, death, exit forbidden: Jews

PLAN:

'Wir haben in diesem Land einen Punkt,

von dem alles Unheil ausgeht:

es ist Warschau.'

ADOLF HITLER

Poland to be Germanized, a colony;
Slavs to be used as German slaves;
Jews are vermin, must exterminate.

O, Angel of death, dark being of terror
we huddle beneath your wings,
sleep happed about with rags, no food, no fire.
Our unwashed bodies are pressed close
for warmth, yet these sticks of bones
can give no heat, hardly totter to our tomb.

A German woman's punished in the street.
Her head is shaved.
She wears a notice round her neck;
her crime's engraved.

'I am the very worst of swine,
vile, depraved.
I let my children commit a filthy crime.
They played with slaves.'

This incident is recorded with a photograph in *I Saw Poland Suffer*: A Polish Doctor, Lindsay Drummond, London 1941.

THE SOLUTION

THE SOLUTION

Chelmno 1941.
First 'experiments' were held.
1942 Treblinka, Sobibor, Belzec,
special chambers have been devised
as part of the plan, and vast extensions
are being made in Auschwitz
where, within a single day,
fifteen thousand people
                         undesirables, gypsies, Jews,
can be consumed.
Resistance groups leak the news,
but little interest is aroused.
So the work goes on, and totals rise.
Statistics confuse,
but, remember please —
winter, summer, sun or snow,
fifteen thousand people queue to die.
Did the plan rely
on mere indifference?

Fifteen thousand people die every day.

On the safe side of the fence
peasants rein in their carts
watch trains unload
watch empty wagons shunt away.

. . . HOLY THINGS ARE OVERTHROWN

The God of Moses, Isaac, Jacob,
of burning bush, or cloven stone,
has not come down to save us.
We prayed, and die alone.

Booted feet break last doors open,
holy things are overthrown.
No voice is raised to help us.
No light breaks through the gloom.

Synagogues topple in ruins,
ancient plate is melted down.
Pious lips force out shamed spittle;
beards are plucked out, sidelocks shorn.

Guards search in young men's trousers,
hoist a rabbi's robes.
We fast, we weep: O, Israel:
nothing can atone.

THEY BUILD THE WALLS

It is finished.
La commedia e finita.
It is the end of everything.
The play is ended, the masks are down,
and who is now the hero, who the clown?
Every nightmare, every fear,
every unleashed horror happens here,
behind these walls.
Now each uncensored, savage fairy tale,
each destructive demon is revealed
where entrance is forbidden — *sh'ma Israel* —
(Shema — hear, O Israel)
to Aryan stock,
and escape can be
only into a desert, into lion's jaws.
Nowhere now is safe
for those forced to wear the Judaic star
to read the signs
Juden eintritt verboten.
Juden nicht erwunscht.

Runaway children, savage, starved,
are shot on sight.
Passers-by glance once, then quickly look the other way.

No work, no home, no place to play.
Safer, far safer, to stay
within permitted confines.
Norway, Holland, Belgium fall,
Paris gives way.

All avenues of help are closed. Protest is vain;
only the voice of poetry cries out frustration, pain:
'And what can I tell him, I, New Testament Jew
waiting two thousand years for the return of Christ?
Uncircumcised, I aid his death.'

The quotation comes from a poem by Czesław Miłosz, see Notes.

WE ORGANIZE OUR WALLED-IN LIFE

Enclosed, we organize
canteens and care,
yet hunger grows.
Within our walls
wild children howl,
lie down and die.
Typhus, TB, hunger, stalk
our streets. We stumble
over corpses
at every corner where we walk.
We barter, thieve, trade, beg.
We want to live. We learn the rules,
take off our caps, and school
our bodies to bend
low, low, low
before sticks and blows.
Our guards have the right
to shoot on sight.
They shoot with cameras too,
metres of film, all untrue.
Yet we still pray and celebrate
Passover, remember the exodus;
linen and bread and herbs are spread,
while we weep for our beloved dead.
Fela and her little girls
shed bitter tears, remembering the home they've left,
the father shot, the baby's fevered death.

Jakub Traube sings Hagada, rocking to and fro
recalling the blows which killed his brother
when soldiers had their fun.
Others have already 'disappeared'.
Already 'executions' have begun.
B'shona haba b' jerushalaim.

Hagada is the retelling of the sacred Passover events.
B'shona haba . . . : 'next year in Jerusalem'.

WORK, WORK . . .

But we work. Everyone wants to work. Work
is the only way for Jewish slaves to live,
the only way to buy
foods, passports, protect our families.
We work in factories for German gain,
huge enterprises based in Berlin.
We work while executions multiply.
We work for fear that we too shall be shot,
our twitching bodies left to rot
(later they'll bury people still alive
and seal the pit with lime,
hundreds of deaths every time).

In 1942 the end begins.
The date is the 22nd of July.
Selection starts.
Now we work for fear of transportation
'further east'
in sealed trucks
without suitcases, food,
our destination,
we're told, Siberian wastes.

The Jewish question is already sealed.
Warsaw Jewry is scheduled for Treblinka.

SLAUGHTER

SMUGGLING

Smuggling is the only way now to survive.
Jewish, Polish, even German police connive,
turn, at times, a deliberate, unseeing eye,
take bribes,
as ghetto children clamber up the walls —
though many Jewish children meet their death this way.
The Jewish underworld with contacts, lies,
helps ghetto dwellers stay alive.
Liquidation is thus postponed by the black marketeer,
and men who daily put on their prayer shawl
are saved by shady dealers who heed no law.
Diaries, documents, pay full due
to smugglers of all ages, sorts;
beyond question brave.
'The walls they breach
in search of basic food
are only too likely to become their grave.'[1]
Jewish–Polish relations,
often strained,
dramatically improve,
as both sides strive
against hunger, danger, machine-gun fire.
Yet food brought in at risk of life
can only be used
by those who can afford to pay,
barter, trade.
Beggars, sick and old, starve,
die in droves;
but smuggled food keeps factory slaves
arbeits-faehig, active
in spite of diseases, bereavement, fear.

Death is never more than a shouted word, a levelled arm away.

WHAT CAN'T BE CONQUERED

A self-styled leader,
mean-lipped, black-moustached.

A strong jowled bulldog
with a fat cigar.

A woman who trades
bed linen, cooking-pots
for flour, soap, bread,
risks being imprisoned, shot.

A ragged child
who climbs guarded walls,
crawls through holes
with pockets full
    of potatoes
more costly than gold;
who risks beatings, death.

A Jewish smuggler can't be conquered by anyone.

The black humour of the Ghetto is recorded in
several accounts, but everyone is unanimous in
praising the bravery of smugglers on both sides of
the wall, not least the children who risked death
to bring potatoes to their starving families. The
Ghetto chronicler and archivist, Emanuel
Ringelblum, notes that smuggling marks a new
departure in the history of Polish—Jewish relations.

TREBLINKA

Not a well-known place,
not marked on a major map;
might be classed a bit of a dump;
a one-horse railroad station

where death trains stop each day.

Don't look for a buffet here;
nor a newsagent's stand.
You won't find a porter, either,
nor any ticket-seller.

(Return tickets are not for sale, in any case.)

Everything hushes here,
even three stunted pines,
and the battered sign
which spells out a name:

Look again at those letters:
T R E B . . . and see
instead a secret order:
Get out here to die.

I have based this poem on my translation of *Mała
Stacja Treblinka* by Władyslaw Szlangel, a popular
poet who died in the Ghetto Uprising, April 1943.

RABBI YECHIEL

'The world has never seen such scenes . . .
Every crime in history pales into insignificance with this.'
ABRAHAM LEWIN[1]

Terror mounts. Secretly, in twos and threes,
artists, writers, rabbis meet to celebrate
(age-old Jewish way which makes slaves great).
Hebrew, Yiddish words, banned exalted, free,
punctuate the horror pressing all around.
Past pogroms are recalled. Actors read
Bialik's *Slaughter*. The room is tense. Oh, now heed
cries of 'How long? How long?' The very ground,
dumb earth, questions the sullen sky.
Wilno, Lublin. A whole nation dies.
Blood of babies, desecration, official lies:
Familien nicht getrennt.

Rabbi Yechiel[2] presides. His listeners note
polished shoes, his personal worth, brave speech.
'Hope against hope. Surely a limit must be reached?'
Protest is cleanliness, a well-cut coat.

Rabbi Yechiel hopes to escape deportation,
takes a factory job, a tool for Hitler's ends.
Classified as something worse than vermin
Jews survive only to serve the Master Nation.
Even here the S.S. seek 'volunteers'.
'Workers for Smolensk.' A random round-up occurs.
Rabbi Yechiel shows the officer stamped papers.
'Sir, I am unfit to travel, being over fifty years . . .'
'Unfit to travel — means: fit to die!' The officer knows
the rules, takes out his pistol, shoots
Rabbi Yechiel's defenceless head. *'Blut!*
Die Bestie blutigt!' This show,
kicking, contempt is the Rabbi's epitaph.
His crumpled corpse is trampled like a leaf.

MUSIC IN THE GHETTO

On Leszno Street a pre-war picture-house
becomes a concert hall. The Ghetto's full
of melodies which shine across each pool
of black despair. Beggars tout tunes to ease
their hunger. Trades, ballads disappear
as, promised bread, families volunteer
for 'journeys further east'; are first to hear
the gas. Can music sweeten nightmares, fear;
do more than rabbi, cantor, psalm or God?
'Ave Maria, young maid full of grace . . .'
Defying censorship, a solo voice
soars clear and strong. Violins shiver, sob.
Her listeners weep, last accolade of tears.
The death camp ends her songs, her eighteen years.

The soloist was Maria Eisenstadt. Her conductor was
Szymon Pulmon. Both were rounded up in the first wave of
deportations in July 1942, and are thought to have perished
in Treblinka. The story is told by Janina Bauman in *Winter
in the Morning*, Virago Press, 1986.

NO WAY TO PUT INTO WORDS

'There is no way to put into words what happened to us.'
A WOMAN CALLED ZIMMERMAN, A MEAT TRADER

The action called 'resettlement' first took three weeks:
three weeks of horror, murder, hell,
tragedies impossible to conceive,
impossible to tell.
Five, six thousand people every day
were herded into trucks, taken away.
Parents hid babies, toddlers in baggage packs,
sedated them, stored them on their backs,
hid underground, in cellars, walled-off rooms,
attics, cupboards without water, food,
listening, every nerve raw, jangling, tense,
as relentless boots tramped across creaking floors
kicked open flimsy doors.
Fists shattered glass, tore chairs apart,
punched victims outside. We heard their screams,
heard pistol shots, machine-gun fire.
Jewish blood rinses our streets in streams,
spatters on walls. The angel of death
invades our blood-smeared doors.
Earth, do not hide your face from our blood
nor turn deaf ears to our cries.

The events on this and the following two pages are based on
an extract from the diary of Natan Zelichower,[1] who
survived the loss of his wife and daughter, Stella, was
transported in April 1943 to Buchenwald, continued to
write his diary, returned to Poland in 1945 and donated his
papers to the Jewish Historic Commission in Krakow.

O, GOD, THEY'RE HERE!

I stood on guard between broken attic boards,
saw a hand reach out, a head appear.
        O, God, they're here!
I couldn't breathe. Starving, weak,
I fainted. My wife and children shake me, speak.
'It's over now. They've gone.'
I nodded. No words, dumb.
'We're safe . . . but mother. No . . .'
She was too weak to hide. 'Go,
save yourselves,' she said.
They shot her as she lay in bed.

No words. Guilt, horror, hatred, fear.
And yet the need to save ourselves,
        get documents
listen to official lies,
scrabble among our ruined lives.
I went to work. Next day they closed the gates.
We heard shouts, a hellish hue and cry we knew
so well: the rounding up of hunted Jews.
They said, workers would be safe. They said . . .
What does it matter what they said?
We scattered like field mice
clustered round each threatened sheaf
while sickles slice the harvest through.
My family's attic nest
has been ransacked by well-armed rats.

I run to Umschlagplatz.
This is where the final choice is made.
A Jewish guard tries to make me comprehend,
presses a crumpled note into my hand.
I read: Daddy, do your best
to find us. We're lost,
Mummy and I are scheduled for the waiting train
but maybe fate will be kind,
and we'll all go home again.

No words, no words to describe my pain.

HIDING-PLACE

1.

New notices: '*Selection. Every Jew*
must make his way to places named below
to be informed who still may work, whose lot
is liquidation.' We choose rather to squat
in stinking drains. I find a bookcase, shove
it to a wall, and make a space where twelve
may hide. We spend three days inside. Bad air.
Then soldiers clear the house, march up the stair.
The emptied rooms are thick with horror, fear.
A woman. 'Let me live. I give you, sir . . . '
'*Gut, komm* . . . Now run. It's safe.' She turns. His gun's
stacatto ends her flight. His business done,
he steps across her body into night.
Behind our wall of books we wait, stiff, mute.

2.

We wait. Lilka coughs. '*Hans komm. Hier sind*
noch Juden.' Booted feet pound by. We dare
not move; we choke with fear; but now the air
is torn apart. A baby yells. '*Ein Kind!*
Verflucht noch mal!' A window rasps. They throw
the squaller out. No more noise now. They leave.
Doors bang. It's safe to stretch, to cough, to breathe.
We do not stir. We feel that fall, feel so
appalled, so lost. Because that baby cried
we live – to share the guilt, the murder; seek
the child among scattered bodies, weak
with horror as we witness how they died,
each one debased by terror. Silent screams
stamp anguish on our faces, haunt our dreams.

UMSCHLAGPLATZ

Every hour, every day —
is no longer an hour
is no longer a day
It is a sacrifical altar prepared within your bones.
SUTZKEVER

This is the place. Selection has been made.
People are sorted, anguished and afraid.
We sold our clothing, wedding rings, procured
what food we could. All we have now is stored
in rucksacks. Ignorant of their design,
exterminate: make Warsaw *Judenrein*,
we stand in July heat, September rain,
like patient cattle board each waiting train.
We have no choice. They beat and shoot. Our route,
defined by death, is mapped. Our minds are numb
with grief, bereavement, hunger. We still long
to build another life, sing proper songs
for those we dared not mourn. New horrors come.
The engine jolts. We travel to our fate.

LINKS – RECHTS

We go together. Mother holds my hand
lest we're lost in this huge crowd,
turmoil and tragedy. Old, sick, starved folk
force bowed backs straight,
march past the guards, look strong, fit, brave.
(And who is now the conqueror, who the slave –
the Gestapo, with whips and guns, harsh commands,
who hold the fate of each poor victim in their hands?)
'*Halt! Weiter!* Wait!'
A soldier pulls out
a bent old man, a pretty girl,
although it is forbidden to contaminate
the *Herrenvolk – Rassenschande!*
Another soldier separates
a mother from her pre-school child.
Despair punctuates our progress to the fenced-off square,
where a pointed hand, rasping voice make final choice.
Links – means to the trains,
rechts – we may return
to the Ghetto, barbed wire, executions, fear;
yet each of us longs for this.

Mother tugs my hand. 'Child, if they choose me
for the train, don't you come too.'
Her lips are dry. Sweat shines on her taut skin.
Her breath is foul. I know she is in pain.
'I'm forty,' she goes on, 'sick and done,
but you are young.'
What can I say? I only know
my heart pounds with relief and joy.
Mother won't mind if I let her die!

So we walk on. Horses pull
carts piled high with luggage. We watch with fear.
It's certain sedated children are stowed inside.
A sentry shouts. Cases fall. Horses rear.
More gunfire, blows. I crumple to my knees,
and when I look again, mother isn't here.
The soldiers have taken my mother away.
'Du, Maedchen . . .' So now I am to be controlled.
Ahead walk such pretty girls. The soldier stares,
holds out his hand. *'Links.'*
They turn towards the square.
I tremble. I am stunted, undergrown.
I listen for the voice I dare not disobey.
'Rechts,' he says, *'rechts! Geh!'*
and waves me on.

From an account by Stefania Szochur. See also the poem
'Stefania'. Stefania Szochur survived the Ghetto and
subsequent deportation and became an actress in the Jewish
theatre in Warsaw.

GEIPEL

And in the air the sound of bitter weeping;
Holy God, why are you silent, sleeping?[1]

'How do you like our plan of action;
a good idea, what, this selection?'

'Looking forward to your holiday?
You'll get nice work to do, a little pay.'

Geipel patrols courtyards, searches flats,
pays punctillious attention
to those who have been rounded up at Umschlagplatz.

He chats to a young woman,
chucks her toddler under chin:
'Lovely young chap, bonny, good as gold.

'Give him this piece of bread.'
'Oh, thank you, sir!' The woman turns.
High on her shoulder shines her child's contended head.

Geipel takes out his pistol, aims.
The mother's shoulder carries one red stain.

Visits done,
Geipel thinks of pleasure.
'*Du, Maedchen*, blue-eyed, lovely one . . . '

Huge eyes gaze at his gun
a long, long pause; she's paralysed, dumb.

'. . . A Jew like you, whose eyes are blue!'
He aims between her eyes, and shoots.

Her father, an old man, runs
to his daughter, rocks her body in his arms.

'I selected her for fun before bed.
I like it better now she's dead.
Leave her, she's mine.

'Stand up!' The old man stands,
may not ignore his lord's commands.

'You know that I can shoot you too;
but, see, I'm merciful. Now go.'

He turns away, stooped, slow.

And Geipel's bullet whistles through his brain.

   z'kor yah rachamekha wa hasadekha . . .[2]
   Remember thy loving-kindness, O Lord.

Geipel's crimes are described by Samuel Puterman, whose
account also recorded the fate of Nuchem Lejbkorn and his
tragic song (see 'Night'), together with the story of Passover
in the Ghetto ('We organize our walled-in life'), of the burial
of living people ('Work, work . . .') and other details which
went to make these poems. See also Notes.

I COULD NOT BLESS THIS WORLD
AT WAR

A marvellous summer moon
illumines hopeless streets.

I shall be vapour soon.

Death harvests all we are,
earth, water, air.

To be born, to live — we learn;
may we not learn to die?
And, after death, what then?

Every step we take is fraught
with death. Each dying child I touch
teaches me death needs time and thought.

But last night in my prayer,
though I felt well-being stir,
I could not bless this world at war.

I sat quietly, breathing deep,
feeling muscles, mind relax
amidst children in untroubled sleep.

Yet the blessing would not come.
My upraised hands grew slack.
I was powerless and dumb.

Without blessing, healing will not come.

Dr Janusz Korczak (Henryk Golszmit),[1] writer, doctor and broadcaster, devoted his life to orphan children and their rights, defending delinquents in the courts. It was thought Korczak's orphanage would survive the deportations, but the children were ordered to march to the death trains. Korczak resisted every effort of his Polish friends to save him, and amazed frantic deportees and police alike with the calm way he led the children on to the train.

CHILDREN SING KADDISH

No birds fly in the ghetto;
no flower grows.
Pavements are crowded, hunted:
blood daily flows.

Only the cemetery pulsates
with living things.
A cow is bartered among the graves;
birds still sing.

Unnamed dead lie exposed;
new-dug earth waits.
S.S. men bring girls in furs
to see the sight.

Now, towards older stones,
children come,
following a bearded man
to sing their hymn.

Those who weep among new graves
find comfort in old prayers.
Children's voices; the worn black book —
these reassure.

Closely wrapped in folds of prayer
the man stands so still
that sparrows flutter to his hands,
settle on his shawl.

Birds and children trust their saint
who begs their food,
sits beside dying beggar children,
protects his brood.

Protects, but cannot save them,
in the July attacks.
Singing, boards the cattle wagons,
receives the gas.

Dr Janusz Korczak died in Treblinka with the children in his care.

LOVE IN THE GHETTO

Zula is fifteen. Her soft hair
is shot with light. She wears
a braided crown above
a heart-shaped face; wistful eyes —
which make her parents fear
for her safety when vicious guards
march near. They do not know
Zula has a lover, Leon, three years
older, who longs to unbraid his sweetheart's hair,
longs to see her young body bare,
does not yet guess
young girls undress for gas.

Leon's kisses caress her upturned face,
her hands, her dress.
He is passionate and chaste.

They drink coffee, even dance. Zula attends
an illicit school, reads verse
in three languages, learns
a little English. Leon works
for a ghetto magnate; after hours
plants vegetables in marked-out soil
beside the cemetery.
Sometimes Zula says, 'Isn't it wrong
to waltz when children starve?
I didn't eat any lunch the other day.
I gave it to a beggar child, but, Leon,
that's giving food to only one.
There are so many starving folk, and none
of us ever really has enough to eat these days.'
'We can only try to do the best we can,
and you're an angel.'

Leon's kisses sweeten Zula's pain.

One day Leon doesn't come
to the coffee shop at their usual time.
When Zula meets him next, he grabs her hand,
hustles her into a blacked-out room.
'Kept dark by order; it's too near the Pawiak.'
'The prison?' she asks. He nods.
'Executions, chases with dogs trained
to savage those who wear the armband.'
Zula stares. His face is hard.
'So why have you brought us here?'
His mouth silences hers, his hands
explore her breasts, tear open her dark dress.
She knows she must resist.
'Love me now,' he begs. 'We can't love when we're dead.'
'We're young,' she soothes. 'You can't really mean . . .'
'I want you, Zula.' 'No, it isn't right. I'm scared.'
'Nothing's right. Oh, Zula, if you knew what I've seen;
Don't you understand?
Bit by bit they're killing us.'

When they next meet
Leon is wearing the uniform of the Jewish police,
is herding families into the street, has found
women whose bodies blur
the sight of too many naked dead,
has found a way, he thinks, to stay alive.

He is sweating in the July sun;
Zula trembles with memories she can't express.
'I might have had his child. No, no;
his eyes are cruel.'

She is swept towards a waiting train:

Space for forty cattle within.

Anguish ends her dream.

... FOR THOSE WHO DIE AS CATTLE

Throughout the summer people are marched here —
some fifteen thousand is the daily score.
They bring their luggage, but so vast the crowd
a bare six kilos only is allowed.
So people throw clothes, towels, soap away;
still hope they'll work, buy, sell, not die.
Some needs must still be met. There is no place,
herded like beasts, no privacy, no space.
The butcher guards crack whips, kill weaklings, curse,
stamp useless passports, mock, make torment worse.
Trucks come, and people push on board. The sides
are sealed. Sentries guard the roof with guns.
The route is secret. Drivers dare not tell:
the plan's conceived from start to end in hell.

TRANSPORT

Impossible to escape
this sealed place;
we stand to sleep.
No food, no space.

People lose sanity,
suffocate;
delirious, betray
names, dates;

prophesy our fate
with eldritch prayers,
lament our unsung dead,
rave, swear.

Even those who endured
untold torture
cannot withstand
this last nightmare.

Trucks rattle. Bodies sway.
This rhythmic clack
spelt holiday,
parents, picnic box.

Soon all that we possess
will be stripped from us.
We'll stand in nakedness
beneath the gas.

They'll stuff our hair in mattresses,
put us to use:
as lampshades, handbags, soap,
recycle us.

NO ESCAPE

No escape — unless you pull
with naked hands
filthy floorboards, push
rotting corpses, make
a gap through which those left behind
can glimpse railway lines, feel
the rush of air, smoky as dragon's breath.
Then it is necessary
to ease your starved, stiff body down;
hang between the flying tracks and jump.

Some end so, flung beneath the relentless wheels.
Others fall prey to guards who lie across the roof;
are hurt, break bones, are shot,
lie crippled by the track
at the mercy of dogs, wolves, police.
A few make it to the woods,
live hunted lives.

BESIDE THE RAILWAY

Two men, a woman jumped.
The men died instantly, shot by the guards.
Their bodies lay beside the track.
The woman broke her leg, dragged herself up here —
a villager relates, one of those daredevil types.

It was all too obvious who she was, though no one spoke.
She found her voice first, asked us if those others lived.
We told her, no.
It was broad daylight, an open place.
Word soon got round.

People came and went. I was the only one to stay.
She asked me if I'd help her. 'Not hide me,
of course not, only could you bring
something to ease the pain? Look, I've money here,'
she said, trying to reach inside her skirt.
Money — well, it was the middle of the war,
but still, I didn't want to take cash from the likes of her.
I brought her vodka, cigarettes.
I mean, anyone would have done the same.

She sat up, cradled her injured leg,
sorted her skirt. She'd cut her hands,
I saw. I noticed blood;
noticed her eyes, too, lashes long and dark.
Folk stood around. Still no one spoke.
An old woman wrapped in shawls bent low,
almost it seemed like she was on her knees.
She put a cup between those bloodstained hands,
gave bread.

Later two policemen came. 'I jumped,' she confessed.
'You'd better shoot me yourselves.'
That shook them! They backed away.
'You've baffled the cops,' I told her,
and I too bent, held vodka to her mouth,
lit her cigarette.
'It's cold,' she commented.
'Ah, spring's slow this year. Did you know those guys,
the ones they shot?'
'My husband.'
'Oh; didn't make it, then?'
Her eyelids closed. 'No,
but he was luckier than me, all the same.'
'Drink up,' I said.
She drank, and dozed.

People still came and went.

'It's getting dark,' I said,
and watched them drift towards their blink of fire,
soup, bed.

The policemen returned.
'You'll have to shoot me this time,' she said,
and hid her dark-lashed eyes.

'You do it. No, you.'

My voice was firm. 'I'll do it, sirs.'
I saw her lashes move,
knew that she watched me take that gun.
I knelt, bent low.

What else was there to be done?

Orders were given late next day
to take those bodies away:
hers and the other two beside the railway.

This poem is based on a prose account by Zofia Naulkowska[1]
who interviewed victims and witnesses of war crimes.

AFTER THE
SELECTION
OCTOBER – DECEMBER
1942

UNIFORMS FROM THE EASTERN FRONT

They deliver to their Jewish workforce Nazi uniforms –
three hundred thousand: the tally of last winter's fight
in Russia's relentless frost. Husbands, fathers, sons.
These German dead bring hope to Jewish slaves. And yet
our fate is so completely bound up with the Master-race
that their defeat is likely to be our loss,
for our right to existence depends on how we serve
the war effort which has determined we shall not survive.
We launder, disinfect, repair;
find in this mess things which belong to us:
Warsaw haberdashery, robbed by the S.S.,
even Jewish prayer shawls stolen from our dead.
And so, by odd coincidence, bitter justice:
these plundered talliths return to us.
We read letters from the Fatherland. Life is not easy
    there;
while the black mood
of letters from the Front give us ambiguous cheer.
Smiling photographs of Heinrich, Hans,
contradict the filth and blood,
louse-ridden, muddied stuff. Lice!
The Ghetto is rich enough in that commodity.
We do not need
to import this merchandise.

So we recycle battlegear for armies to murder us.

AFTER THE SELECTION

After the Selection the Ghetto shrinks inside.
The only children left are 'criminals' we hide,
who have no right to breathe or make a noise.
Each new blockade contorts their faces, eyes.

There are few women; no one to cook or clean.
How did they do it, we wonder; wishing we had seen
the marvel that mothers laundered without soap,
and without provisions served us soup.

We have no family life; we are truly slaves.
Our children were snatched from us; they stole our wives.
Only work is left for us, without food, or pay;
yet without this work we're all earmarked to die.

RUMOUR

Rumour is our daily food. It wasn't true,
they say, about Treblinka, in spite
of that legendary Jew who got away
with news of naked corpses,
too many to be buried; wagon loads of clothes.
Our families, they say, really have gone 'further east'.
So-and-so got a letter, stamped, postmarked with a date,
saying how well his relatives are doing.
They work, and do not starve.
Ask him. He'll let you read the very words.

Another rumour spreads that the children have returned:
two thousand pale children
have come back home.

It is known that grief deceives; that in a crowded street
a mother may greet her departed child,
then turn away, confused.
Ah, little lost ones, you are ghosts,
come back here to haunt us, who have lost all hope.
I think that when the tale of our tragedy is fully told;
grieving Jewish parents will hold out waiting arms
to welcome long lost children, white as Russian snow,
fair and strong as birches, hair shining in the sun:
then turn away in sorrow, deluded by a dream.

For our children are dust and ashes
who visit us in sleep,
dance in every sunbeam
fade away in rain,
sting our eyes like snowflakes
soft and sharp as tears.
This is the truth we chronicle,
this is our only heir.

These three poems have come from the diary of Emanuel
Ringleblum, who like Lewin was determined that some witness
should remain. See Notes for further details of Dr Ringelblum's
remarkable work.

RESISTANCE
JANUARY – MAY
1943

RESISTANCE

In death the bitter truth is: life goes on.
We leave a silent, curtained room,
and step into the traffic's roar;
order flowers, food, a car;
turn from grave or urn
to find children playing, snow, sun.

Each small normality
strikes like a blow between the eyes;
yet these things reassure –
at least, in normal times.

Here death has become too commonplace;
every day is squalid, mean,
an unvoiced scream.

Hunger wakes us early; first thoughts
are filled with fear.
We gulp back bile, anguished, ill.
Every person here
has lost those who are most dear.
We make forays into plundered rooms
for mouldy food no one now owns.

Our route lies always underground,
or through holes cut in adjoining walls
throughout the beleaguered town.

The death penalty awaits
any who go through the ghetto gates.
Yet a few families escape, those who
may pass as Polish, venerate the cross,
forget their Jewish names,
pay their way with diamonds, wedding rings,

a kiss on Aryan mouth or hands,
somehow win a moment's grace.

Polish friends, former employees, priests, nuns,
help, hide – the fear is always:
someone may betray.
Peasants milk thin cows for runaways,
or kill on sight.
Underground fighters debate:
should Jews have arms? And Jews themselves well know
a single Nazi death means: exterminate,
murder which in its turn produces
nothing,
no echo of protest abroad.
Thus resistance is paralysed.

IT IS WRITTEN

Already, of the 370,000 inhabitants of the
Warsaw Ghetto before July 1942, only 70,000
survive. And on 18 January 1943 a new wave of
liquidation begins. The diarist Abraham Lewin is
one of those who died.

He loved the Book of Books,
loved poetry, Hebrew, learning,
loved Luba his wife, his daughter;
was great of mind and heart,
passionate for people.

Hunted from house to house,
he collects careful information,
notes springtime, summer, slaughter,
records the whole horror of Selection,
implores God for a reason;
sees through every fabrication:
writes: 'European Jewry is scheduled for extermination.'

'BROTHERS, FIGHT!'

Had Lewin survived he would have noted, as
others observed, that this time the Jews do not go
to their slaughter without protest.

Young people read graffiti scrawled
by now dead fingers on hidden walls:
Brothers, fight!

Gaunt nuns[1]
come to the ghetto walls
with bread and guns.

Work passes, stamps no longer hypnotise;
No one now flees
from street to street
in desperate trust
that this block won't be so dangerous.

We have seen too many corpses
thrown into uncovered carts.

Shooting begins.

Starving boys and girls with hand grenades
resist machine-gun fire.
Polish and Jewish flags now wave
above the Ghetto. Poles outside
report amazed: Germans flee.

Tanks roll in.
The first three tanks do not return.
The Ghetto starts to burn.
Choked with smoke, shot down, resisters fight fires.

'Raise the alarm throughout the world,'
announces the Polish underground.
'Appeal to Churchill. Tell the Pope.
Save us. Our fate is in your hands.'

TOP SECRET

On 16 February 1943 Himmler[1] orders the
destruction of the Ghetto.

The destruction of the Ghetto is essential
to end unrest in Warsaw, stamp out crime.
Five hundred thousand subhumans,
Untermenschen, unfit for use,
must be wiped off the face of the earth;
Warsaw, a constant danger spot,
centre of disorder and rebellion,
will be reduced in size.

Nazi factory owners spread official lies:
'Jewish war workers, go on the transports.
Take your families too.
You will live, survive the war.'

Does our life then depend
on slavish submission to our conquerors' rules?
Propaganda conceals unspoken truth;
the official plan is, as always, death.

Revolt begins.

SHMUEL ZYLBERSTEIN REPORTS

I decide to stay.
I say farewell to relatives, friends.
Who knows where this will end?

My sister's son sits on my knee.
Last April his father hid him in a sack
and carried him from Umschlagplatz.

'Daddy wants us to travel on the train;
promises fresh air, food. Mummy said the same,
but she went to the gas. I know they'll murder us.'

'No, no, it will all end well, you'll see.'
This little boy is wise beyond his five short years.
I kiss goodbye. My eyes, like his, are filled with tears.

Seventeen of us hide; four grenades, seven guns.
'Brothers, get ready!'
I run up to the loft.
Jews are fighting at last! I want to be a part of this.
Soldiers march in. Left, right; left right.
But our boys mow them down. Once more!
Crack! Another hits the ground.
The sight is sweet, best I've seen for years.
I run the whole length of the loft
and out to the Aryan side, hide,
get a phone call through to friends.

'The Ghetto's up in arms,' my friend chokes.
'Kids do battle like heroes. Women fling petrol cans,
holding little babies in their arms.
National banners fly from house nineteen.
Can't talk any more. The house has gone up in flames.
They're forcing people into burning homes.'
His voice crackles across the phone.
'The door's caught now. They're roasting us alive.
Chin up! Hold on! Be brave!'

From my hideout I watch the Ghetto burn.
Twentieth century: behold your shame.

The events in this poem are from the account by Shmuel
Zylberstein,[1] an active member of the Jewish Resistance.
Shmuel Zylberstein's diary records life in the Ghetto, the
author's hair-raising escapes from the Gestapo and his
experiences subsequently in various concentration camps.
These records are found in the Jewish Historical Archives,
but further details of the author's life are not known.

19 APRIL 1943

It is the eve of Hitler's birthday. Five thousand Jews
must report to Umschlagplatz. The transport leaves,
as planned. Now comes this news:
not far from Warsaw the trains are stopped.
Everyone is ordered out.
Snow clings to the fields but spring is in the air.

'Dig your graves!' So, death is to be here,
not Treblinka. Do machine-guns hurt less than gas?
A present for the Fuehrer: five thousand of us.

On April 20 a second transport is due
to celebrate our leader's birthday.
People hide. Searches begin, a hunt for human prey.
Women and children are taken hostage.
But now houses which seemed empty come alive.
Bullets whine. Rooftops explode.
'Candles for our leader's cake. A firework display!'
The S.S. flee.

The news of the railway massacre was brought back to the Ghetto
by some escapees. It spurred resistance in the face of the most
appalling odds and delayed the final destruction of the Warsaw
Ghetto.

GALLOWS HUMOUR

In the sewers two friends meet.
'Have you heard the one about . . .'

'It goes like this:

It was the end. Only two Jews were left,
ropes about their necks, waiting to be hanged.
'Cheer up, it could be worse.'

'Listen, they've been saying that since
the ghetto walls began to rise.'

'I know, but haven't you thought
why they're hanging us; why we're not shot?
They haven't any ammunition left, you see;
the joke's on us, even when we die.'

STEFANIA

When streets become silent
we know death is near;
booted feet on the pavement
closer, closer: what fear!

Stefania looks round and sees
soldiers march close.
So, it's happening to me.
They've caught me at last!

They group us in fours;
shout, shove and curse.
Fill a lad's belly with shot.
He yowls like a cat.

'Take his hands and his feet,
lug him like a beast.
Soon you'll all yell like him.'
They group us again.

The sun hurts our eyes.
I look at the wall;
hear gunfire and cries:
it's the end of us all.

Tanks, troops march in.
They're armed to the teeth.
Now battle's begun
we'll fight to the death.

'Weiter, jetzt, schnell!' –
through streets hot as hell.
A tank's ringed with fire;
we start to cheer.

Our guards push us on
towards Umschlag-square;
load us on a train:
all around us is war.

The train lurches away
towards the unknown.
Fire flares in the sky:
a fiery moon –

O, world, look at that moon,
red, red as our blood.
Remember our doom,
lament our dead.

Stefania was arrested on 19 April 1943
and was deported to a labour camp. She
managed to escape and hid in Warsaw,
helped by two Polish women who took
great risks, for Stefania had no
documents. Eventually she procured
forged papers and worked as a domestic
help with another Polish woman until
the end of the war. Stefania's story is
also told in 'Links – rechts'.

THE GHETTO BURNS

'The light of Israel will become a fire.'
PSALM 107:17

Armed detachments ring the Ghetto round.
Cars with machine-guns, tanks.
Resistance is co-ordinated, planned.
Red Cross vehicles carry off a constant flow
of injured storm troopers.
(Ghetto dwellers, of course, receive no care.)
Fires begin. Incendiaries drop from the air.
Yet the S.S. enter the Ghetto only by day.
At night Jewish fighters beat back Nazi lines.
Combat zones change, attacked by German planes.
Fires spread. By April 28, more than eight days
after fighting began, six thousand troops,
heavily armed, now fight the Jews.
Cellars where fighters hide are flooded out;
sewers blown up with dynamite.
Whole streets are razed. Even guerrillas are amazed:
a city burns to smoke out 'subhuman' slaves.
Specialists analyse: the fires in the Ghetto
are the greatest Europe has ever seen.
Jews issue this appeal: so that the world may know
our nation's pain.

> From smoke and conflagration,
> from ruin and ash,
> slaves of the Ghetto greet you.
> We know you watch our epilogue.
> Our deaths must stir the world.

The world is dumb.
Gunshot still comes in sporadic bursts:
death throes of Poland's Jews.
The Ghetto lies in ruins above the dead.
It is the end.

IN THE SEWERS

They've hunted us from street to street,
now we're forced into basements, cellars,
while flames destroy the rooms
we knew as homes.

Women scream. Children sob, choke.
'The fire's in here.'
Luckily there's water. We soak
clothing, cover hair, lose eyebrows, skin.
Nowhere is safe, yet every bolthole, every den,
conceals someone we know. 'Have you seen . . . ?'
'No, I'm sorry, no.' Voices fade.

'We must dig a tunnel through.'
We have no proper spade,
no map to show the way to go.
We enter a stinking drain, crawl
through unlit slime;
knock against a wall;
smell gas.

And so we cast about,
until the S.S. flood us out.

We hide underground. Every day
one of the boys goes out, skulks around;
we must see what's left in all the rubble;
if food is to be found; above all, if we can,
learn what system of attack our conquerors plan.

Our scout returns.
'The whole place is in ruins. Grey shapes prowl
like wolves, swoop like birds of prey,
croak: "'*Raus, 'raus.*
Alle Juden 'raus!" A few sad wraiths obey.'

How long can we last out?
We dream of escape.

The ways are blocked.
The grapevine, though, holds good.
New folk enter
our hiding-place, bring morsels of food.
There is a hopeful, even a euphoric mood,
talk of getaways in abandoned cars,
of finding families, of the end of war.

Outside in the yard
some woman stands, curses, prays.
Why does she watch this house?

We invite her to share
our hiding-place — safer for her and us.
'Listen,' she sobs, 'somewhere
birds are singing; spring has come.
But here the sky is dumb;
the earth as deaf as stone.

. . . I'd only slipped next door
for food when I heard the fire roar.
The kids were hiding on the second floor.
"Hold on, I'll get you out," I shout.

But the fire was blazing up the stair.
Now they're under all that rubble there.
So I won't come in, thank you all the same.
I'll just stay here and call their names,
so they'll know I love them still.'

In the morning we found
her body on the ground;
knew our hunters had been around,
heard later that a baby's cry
deflected the hunt to a cellar nearby,
where a whiff of warm air was a sign
of human, hidden life crushed tight.
A sign to them to ignite
their charges, set off dynamite.
A sign to us to carry on the fight
though death is closing round us thick as night.
No one will dig our graves. These stinking dens
shall hold unnamed bones.

'In the sewers' is taken from the account by Leon Najberg.
A fourteen year-old at the outset of war, Leon Najberg lost
an elder brother in 1939. His mother and sister were
exterminated in July 1942; his younger brother died in April
1943. Leon Najberg was assigned to an armaments factory
outside the Ghetto. He returned to take part in the
Uprising, and later went into hiding, continuing to write
his memoirs, which are considered to be one of the most
important sources of the Ghetto story, particularly the last
phase of the Ghetto, the desperate fight amongst total ruin.
After the war, Leon Najberg's papers disappeared. He
recalled the entire story from memory and started work
again. In 1958, now resident in Israel, he published his
memoirs, *Aharonim bekce amered shel geto Warsha*.

GENERAL JURGEN STROOP REPORTS
TO HIS COMMANDING OFFICER

16 May 1943.

The Ghetto *Aktion* is at its end.
Es gibt nun keinen judisch' Wohnbezirk
in Warschau mehr. The vermin are destroyed.
We carried out a major, well-planned work.

The last one hundred eighty criminals,
subhuman element's wiped out. The heart
of Polish Jewry ceased to beat. The whole
show ended quarter after six. The part

once known as Ghetto now is closed. We razed
the synagogue. No losses on our side.
We bested even Nero with our blaze!
Fifty-six thousand sixty Jews have died.

I shall submit a detailed document,
statistics, deaths, at our next conference.

TWO ELEGIES

Voices whisper in the mist,
cry in autumn rain;
laugh when sweethearts kiss
bicker like children in the lane

Houses stand where ghetto walls
bounded limitless despair.
It's hard to hear when voices call:
ears, perforce, must close
when want becomes too hard to bear;
and all that's left is loss.

Death struck them day and night,
carried them beyond our sight;

from ransacked houses, fearful streets:
gunfire, blows, booted feet:

musicians, traders, young and old,
scholars, craftsmen, girls with child.

Their lullabies, their stories, dreams,
are turned to rubble which rebuilds homes;

shroud dwelling blocks like autumn mist.
Passers-by may glimpse a fleeting ghost

or hear a whispered word: remember us.

NOTES

Meaning of pain

[1] Abraham Sutzkever, born in Vilnius, now lives in Israel.

[2] See 'A Jewish Cemetery' from Carol Rumens, *Collected Poems*, Chatto.

[3] Zygelboim's note is quoted in *Battle of the Warsaw Ghetto*, S. Mendelsohn, Yiddish Scientific Institute, New York, 1944.

[4] Adam Czerniakow, an engineer, hoped that giving in to some German demands would protect the bulk of Jewry from worse excesses – a policy born out of centuries of persecution. Although some of the Ghetto dwellers, notably E. Ringelblum, condemned Czerniakow, he was generally admired for his efforts to provide welfare and alleviate suffering among the starving sufferers in the Ghetto. His death shook the Ghetto community and is reported to have stunned the Nazis, but the deportation document he refused to sign was implemented anyway.

Night

[1] Isaac Babel, born in Odessa 1894, died in a Siberian concentration camp in 1941. Babel is best known for *Red Cavalry*, a collection of stories set around the civil war and 1920 Cossak campaign against Poland. His play, *Dusk* (1928), portrays Jewish life in Odessa.

[2] All the extracts from Puterman's diary are from *Pamiętniki z getta Warszawskiego*, edited by Michal Grynberg, Panstwowe Wydawnictwo Naukowe, Warszawa, 1988.

Lullaby

[1] 'Raisins . . .': references to Jewish traditional songs.

Tightrope walker

Gabriella's story is recorded with a detail of a drawing, 'Children holding hands', in *Children's Drawings and Poems, Terezin 1942–1944*, Statni Zidovske Museum, Prague, 1959.

A wave of benediction

[1] The title comes from Oscar Miłosz, quoted by his cousin Czesław Miłosz, *Native Realm*, Penguin, 1988.

[2] German Jews wore a yellow star; the Jews of Eastern Europe wore blue.

Ich weiss nicht

As well as the quotes from 'Die Lorelei' by Heinrich Heine, I have referred to: [1] the Book of Ruth 1:16, and [2] 2 Samuel 1:19.

'How old was I . . . ?'

See Kipling's *Puck of Pook's Hill* for an unusually sympathetic portrayal of medieval Jewry.

Medieval ghettos

'*Ido vocabutur getto, quia erant ibi ultra dudecim fornaces et ibi fundabatur aes,*' Senate of Venice, quoted by Dr Manfred Lachs in *The Ghetto of Warsaw*, London, 1942.

They build the walls

'And what can I tell him . . .' This is my translation of lines by Czesław Miłosz, *Biedny chrzecijanin patrzy na getto*, from Głosy biednych ludzi, Czytelnik, Warszawa, 1988.

Smuggling; What can't be conquered

Many chroniclers, notably Ringelblum (see below) record the extraordinary bravery of smugglers on both sides of the war. In Ringelblum's view it marks a new departure in Polish–Jewish relations.
[1] 'The walls they breach . . .' is taken from Henryka Lazowert's popular Polish poem, 'Little Smuggler', quoted in the introduction to Abraham Lewin, *A Cup of Tears*, Blackwell, 1988.

Treblinka

Szlangel's poem is quoted in *Kronika Getta*, Emanuel Ringelblum, Cztetelnik, Warszawa 1988.

Rabbi Yechiel

[1] Abraham Lewin. Like that of his friend, Emanuel Ringelblum, Lewin's diary of the Ghetto was found in milk churns. It is a great and moving record of the annihilation of a people and way of life, of humanity in the midst of daily brutality. Published for the first time in English as *A Cup of Tears* (Blackwell, 1988), it has been translated by Christopher Hutton and edited by Anthony Polonsky. Abraham Lewin lost his wife in the first wave of deportations, but in spite of his grief he went on with his chronicle of daily events. His daughter was saved from Treblinka by getting a job, sorting out the personal property of exterminated families. Abraham Lewin's account finishes on the eve of 1943. He was probably exterminated in the January deportations.

[2] Rabbi Yechiel's story is told in Michael Zylberberg, *A Warsaw Diary 1939–45*, Vallentine Mitchell, London, 1969.

No way . . .; O, God . . .; Hiding-place

[1] Natan Zelichower's account is from *Pamiętniki getta warszawskiego*.

Umschlagplatz

This poem draws on various records in *Pamiętniki*.

Links – rechts

From *Pamiętniki*: the account by Stefania Szochur.

Geipel

[1] From *Pamiętniki*. The quotation, 'And in the air . . .', is also found in *Pamiętniki* – my translation.

[2] Mourner's Kaddish. Authorized Daily Prayer Book of the Hebrew Congregations of the British Commonwealth, translated by the Rev. S. Singer.

I could not bless . . .; Children sing . . .

[1] These incidents from Dr Korczak's life are described in Betty Jean Lifton, *The King of Children*, Chatto and Windus, 1988. Korczak refused to wear the obligatory armband, was arrested and put into

the notorious Pawiak prison, returning shaken and fearful. But his efforts on behalf of the welfare of his children were heroic.

Despite the starvation of the Ghetto, no child in Korczak's care suffered severe malnutrition, although the doctor himself was gravely ill. He organized cultural and religious events in the teeth of terror, and over and above his work with his own orphan children, begging their food, he wandered through the overcrowded Ghetto streets, trying to comfort the abandoned, dying children who were beyond all other help, so that at least they should not die alone.

His attitude to the process of dying anticipates the Hospice movement. There is now an international Janusz Korczak Association. (See M. Zilberberg, Ringelblum, Lewin, and Betty Jean Lifton, *The King of Children*.)

Love in the Ghetto

The only non-factual incident in this book. But it is fictionalized from actual material and is dedicated to another Zula whose dreams of love ended monstrously. (Janina Bauman, *Winter in the Morning*.)

No escape; Beside the railway

[1] Zofia Naułkowska, well-known Polish novelist, was one of a team who conducted interviews with the victims of Nazi atrocities. Her book *Medaliony* (Czytelnik, Warszawa, 1965), retells some of their stories.

Uniforms from the Eastern Front; After the Selection

These poems are based on Ringelblum's diary, *Kronika Getta Warszawskiego*, edited by Eisenback, translated from Yiddish by Rutkowski, Czytelnik, Warszawa, 1988. Emanuel Ringelblum (born 1900 in Galicia) was an internationally known historian and scholar who became an active member of the Jewish Resistance movement within the Ghetto, where he compiled *Ghetto Archives*.

Ringelblum was in Geneva the day before war was declared. He returned voluntarily to Poland to share the lot of his people and quickly began to keep an exact record of events, working with colleagues to give a complete picture of contemporary Jewish life under Nazi occupation.

The material covering the events up to August 1942 was hidden in ten metal boxes and two milk churns. Later, at the end of February 1943, the second part of the *Archives* was similarly hidden. These two parts were discovered during the rebuilding of Warsaw in 1946 and 1950. A third part has never been found.

Ringelblum survived the Ghetto Uprising, and hid underground in a bunker with thirty other people, including his son. The hiding-place was discovered by the Gestapo on 7 March 1944. All the Jews and the Polish owner of the ground were taken to Pawiak prison, where they perished.

Resistance

The Resistance was led by twenty-four-year-old Mordecai Anielewicz. Anielewicz survived the fighting, but his hiding-place was betrayed and he and his friends committed suicide on 10 May 1943, rather than fall into the hands of the S.S.

Ringelblum names some of the girls who took part in the Resistance . . . Stroop, the Nazi leader, ordered a photograph to be taken of Jewish girls caught with ammunition in their hands.

It is written

Details come from the various sources already quoted.

'Brothers, fight!'

[1] 'Gaunt nuns . . .' Anna Borkowska, Prioress of a Dominican convent sheltered Jews, including Resistance leaders Abba Kovner and Jurek Wilner. Both returned voluntarily to their ghetto – Wilner to Warsaw where he perished with Anieliewicz, and Kovner to Vilnius where he led the Partisan movement.

In 1984, presenting Anna Borkowska with the 'Medal of the Righteous among the Nations of the World', Kovner describes his astonishment when a woman dressed in civilian clothes brought grenades to the Ghetto as gingerly as a child cradling a chicken and blessed the fighters, 'God be with you, my dears.' Warsaw survivors recall similar happenings.

Kovner's speech in story and pictures of the presentation of the award is published in *In the land we shared*, a magazine produced in Warsaw in English and Polish to stress mutual Polish–Jewish ties.

Details of the resistance come from *Pamiętniki* and S. Mendelsohn, *Battle of the Warsaw Ghetto*, Yiddish Scientific Institute, New York, 1944.

Top Secret

[1] Himmler's edict is quoted *Pamiętniki z getta warszawskiego*. It took four weeks, not the anticipated three days, to destroy the Ghetto.

Shmuel Zylberstein reports

[1] Zylberstein's memoirs are from *Pamiętniki*.

19 April 1943

From Mendelsohn, *Battle of the Warsaw Ghetto*.

Gallows humour

From *Pamiętniki*.

Stefania

Quoted from *Pamiętniki*.

The Ghetto burns

From Mendelsohn, *Battle of the Warsaw Ghetto*.

In the Sewers; General Jurgen Stroop . . .

From *Pamiętniki*.

A TOUCH OF FLAME

An anthology of contemporary Christian poetry

Compiled by Jenny Robertson

This book brings together more than 100 poems by
contemporary Christian poets. Some are well known.
Many are little known. All deserve wider recognition.

The selection is not confined to 'religious' poems. Its
broad themes offer rich variety: nativity, incarnation,
commonplace, laughter and tears, landscape, beatitude,
way of the cross, resurrection . . . And the poems
themselves touch and delight the reader. They restore to
a hungry world the lost dimension of wonder.

ISBN 0 7459 1509 4

CHRISTIAN HERITAGE CLASSICS

SPIRITUAL AWAKENING
Classic writings of eighteenth-century devotion

Edited by Sherwood Eliot Wirt

The eighteenth century gave birth to some of the giants
of the Christian faith. Here, in one volume, are the great
writings of the day, chosen not only for their historical
significance, but also for a message that still resounds
with truth today. Selections include excerpts from John
Wesley, Rowland Hill, George Whitefield, Jonathan
Edwards, David Brainerd, John Newton, William Penn,
and others.

ISBN 0 7459 1308 3

CHRISTIAN HERITAGE CLASSICS

SPIRITUAL POWER
Classic writings of nineteenth-century spirituality

Edited by Sherwood Eliot Wirt

This selection from the rich heritage of nineteenth-century Christian writing has been specially chosen to represent material that was popular in its day and offers spiritual challenge to the twentieth-century reader. It includes both well-known authors and those who are less well known. Excerpts are included from Dwight L. Moody, Charles Haddon Spurgeon, F. B. Meyer, Thérèse of Lisieux and others.

ISBN 0 7459 1799 2

A selection of top titles from LION PUBLISHING

A TOUCH OF FLAME Jenny Robertson	£3.95	☐
SPIRITUAL AWAKENING Sherwood Eliot Wirt	£4.95	☐
SPIRITUAL POWER Sherwood Eliot Wirt	£5.99	☐
C.S. LEWIS William Griffin	£5.95	☐
GEORGE MACDONALD William Raeper	£5.95	☐
CLEMO: A LOVE STORY Sally Magnusson	£3.95	☐
THE SHADOWED BED Jack Clemo	£3.95	☐
LILITH George MacDonald	£3.99	☐
PHANTASTES George MacDonald	£3.99	☐
SONS AND BROTHERS Elizabeth Gibson	£2.99	☐
TALIESIN Stephen Lawhead	£3.50	☐
MERLIN Stephen Lawhead	£3.50	☐
ARTHUR Stephen Lawhead	£3.50	☐
EMPYRION ONE Stephen Lawhead	£2.95	☐
EMPYRION TWO Stephen Lawhead	£2.95	☐
IN THE HALL OF THE DRAGON KING Stephen Lawhead	£2.99	☐
THE WARLORDS OF NIN Stephen Lawhead	£2.99	☐
THE SWORD AND THE FLAME Stephen Lawhead	£2.99	☐

All Lion paperbacks are available from your local bookshop or newsagent, or can be ordered direct from the address below. Just tick the titles you want and fill in the form.

Name (Block letters) ....

Address ....

....

Write to Lion Publishing, Cash Sales Department, PO Box 11, Falmouth, Cornwall TR10 9EN, England.

Please enclose a cheque or postal order to the value of the cover price plus:

UK: 60p for the first book, 25p for the second book and 15p for each additional book ordered to a maximum charge of £1.90.

OVERSEAS: £1.25 for the first book, 75p for the second book plus 28p per copy for each additional book.

BFPO: 60p for the first book, 25p for the second book plus 15p per copy for the next seven books, thereafter 9p per book.

Lion Publishing reserves the right to show on covers and charge new retail prices which may differ from those previously advertised in the text or elsewhere, and to increase postal rates in accordance with the Post Office.